GICMP SCHOOL OF PROPHETIC INTERCESSION

TRAINING MANUAL

Dwann Holmes

© 2021

By Dwann Holmes

ISBN:

All rights reserved. No portion of this book may be reproduced, stored in a retrieval system, or transmitted in any form or by any means—electronic, mechanical, photocopy, recording, scanning, or other—except for brief quotations in critical reviews or articles, without the prior written permission of the author.

Unless otherwise noted, all scriptures are taken from the King James Version.

Scriptures marked KJV are taken from the KING JAMES VERSION (KJV): KING JAMES VERSION, public domain.

Scripture quotations taken from the Amplified® Bible (AMPC). Copyright © 1954, 1958, 1962, 1964, 1965, 1987 by The Lockman Foundation. Used by permission. www.lockman.org

Scripture quotations marked (NIV) are taken from the Holy Bible, New International Version®, NIV®. Copyright © 1973, 1978, 1984, 2011 by Biblica, Inc.™ Used by permission of Zondervan. All rights reserved worldwide. www.zondervan.com The "NIV" and "New International Version" are trademarks registered in the United States Patent and Trademark Office by Biblica, Inc.™

Scripture quotations marked HCSB are taken from the Holman Christian Standard Bible®, Copyright © 1999, 2000, 2002, 2003, 2009 by Holman Bible Publishers. Used by permission. Holman Christian Standard Bible®, Holman CSB®, and HCSB® are federally registered trademarks of Holman Bible Publishers.

Scripture taken from *The Message*. Copyright © 1993, 1994, 1995, 1996, 2000, 2001, 2002. Used by permission of NavPress Publishing Group.

Scriptures have also been taken from the Bible Gateway website: www.biblegateway.com

Table of Contents

Setting the Foundation
- Objectives
- Introduction
- Curriculum Matrix for the Course

Leading In: Focus on the Facilitator
- Rationale for a Facilitator-Focused Curriculum
- Curriculum Matrix for the Facilitator
- First Reflection
- Course Vision
- Course Planning Guide
- Prayer Points

Preparing the Facilitator to Lead: Focus on the Course
- Module 1 Overview
- Module 2 Overview
- Module 3 Overview
- Module 4 Overview
- Module 5 Overview
- Module 6 Overview
- Module 7 Overview
- Module 8 Overview
- Module 9 Overview
- Module 10 Overview
- Module 11 Overview
- Module 12 Overview

Leading Out: Focus on the Facilitator

    Facilitator's Evaluation

    Final Reflection

SETTING THE FOUNDATION

Objectives

- Provide the tools to facilitate the *GICMP School of Prophetic Intercession* course.
- Impart the power of prophetic intercession and its principles and protocols.
- Encourage reflection and spiritual development through a facilitator-focused curriculum.
- Create a vision, planning guide, and prayer points for the training.
- Implement an effective facilitation model used in training prophetic intercessors.

Introduction

Blessed be the L<small>ORD</small> my strength
which teacheth my hands to war,
and my fingers to fight: My goodness,
and my fortress; my high tower,
and my deliverer; my shield,
and he in whom I trust;
Psalm 144:1-2a (KJV)

There will be no breaching of walls,
no going into captivity, no cry
of distress in our streets.
Psalm 144:14b (NIV)

In war movies, there is often a scene where a high-ranking official has the soldiers surrounding a table to survey a layout of a planned attack. This battle plan is either on paper or in a 3D model. It shows the strategic actions needed to guard the terrain, avoid the enemy's counterattacks, and secure the victory. This official debriefs the soldiers and trusts them to execute the mission with precision and accuracy. Boot camps and prior battles have trained them in the principles and protocols of warfare. They now know to be ready and stay in position. The troops head out on their mission with their leader's vision to guide them.

As Solomon stated several times in the book of Proverbs, there is nothing new under the sun. What happens in the earth is but a shadow of the things that take place above. The Lord of Hosts excels in the art of strategic warfare as He commands Heaven's armies and dispatches His angels to provide support in spiritual battles. His army functions in rank, order, and protocol. Jehovah Sabaoth enlists prophetic intercessors to serve Him in this militaristic endeavor. He has equipped them with the armor and weapons needed to overcome the enemy.

The Bible records stories of prophets, prophetic intercessors, and leaders who triumphed over opposition because of their dependence on God. Moses and Joshua dealt with external and internal warfare as they led the Israelites, while Gideon learned that much power and victory could flow through what man considered as the least.

David entered every battle with the spiritual intel that the Lord was his buckler and shield, while Elijah and Elisha spoke truth to power and served as vessels from which God's miracles flowed. Deborah judged and prophesied with divine wisdom, while Jael served as a secret weapon to defeat the enemy. Esther used the spiritual weapons of fasting and prayer to deliver her people from national genocide. Each leader consulted the Lord for guidance as they committed their plans unto Him (Prov.16:3).

The Song of Moses refers to the Lord as a man of war (Exo.15:3), while David exalts Him as Jehovah Gibbor in Psalm 24:8-10:

> Who is this King of glory? The LORD strong and mighty, the LORD mighty in battle. Lift up your heads, O ye gates; even lift them up, ye everlasting doors; and the King of glory shall come in. Who is this King of glory? The LORD of hosts, he is the King of glory.
>
> *Selah.* (emphasis added)

Prophetic intercessors can rest in the Lord because He is the greatest military strategist. He knows how to win. His ways and thoughts are higher, and His love is stronger than death. As a facilitator, you can find strategies for prophetic intercession and blueprints for victory in His word. Seek the Holy Spirit for instructions on how to carry out His agenda and train the intercessors that He has entrusted to you.

The *GICMP School of Prophetic Intercession Training Manual* will assist you in your facilitation of the course. It serves two purposes:

(1) a **curriculum** to direct your focus, assist your planning, and guide your reflection. It includes the following:
- Rationale for a Facilitator-Focused Curriculum
- Curriculum Matrix for the Facilitator
- First Reflection
- Course Vision
- Course Planning Guide
- Prayer Points
- Facilitator's Evaluation
- Final Reflection

(2) a **guide** to help you lead your ministry through the training by mapping out the course in a curriculum matrix and providing module overviews that include the following:
- Objectives
- Key Terms, Concepts, and Scriptures
- Lesson Structure and Discussion Questions
- Module Assignment and Rubric
- Facilitation Strategies and Supplemental Exercises

This manual emphasizes **discussion, application, self-assessment, practice**, and **reflection** as key tools in your facilitation of this course. It is highly recommended that you and your ministry keep journals during this training. Let's begin by reviewing the curriculum matrix for the course.

Curriculum Matrix for the Course

\multicolumn{5}{c}{GICMP School of Prophetic Intercession}				
TOPICS	**MODULES**	**CONCEPTS**	**ASSIGNMENTS**	**ASSIGNMENT OUTCOMES**
PROPHETIC INTERCESSION BASICS	**Module 1** Prophetic Intercession 101	Prophetic Prophet Prophetic Intercession W.I.P. Model	1-Page Report	Understand the difference between regular intercession and prophetic intercession.
	Module 2 The Lifestyle of a Prophetic Intercessor	Faith Consecration Intimacy with God Purity of Heart Holiness Yielding to the Holy Spirit Submission	Self-Assessment Action Plan Application	Assess their lifestyles as prophetic intercessors. Identify challenges of prophetic intercession and ways to increase strength and stamina. Analyze the lifestyle of a prophetic intercessor in the Bible.
SPIRITUAL WARFARE STRATEGIES	**Module 3** Prophetic Intercession in Worship Part 1	Declaration/Decree The Power of Prophetic Worship Prophetic Worship as a Bridge & Weapon Spiritual Communion Spiritual Intelligence	Prophetic Prayer	Create a prophetic prayer for a current event or personal situation.

SPIRITUAL WARFARE STRATEGIES (CONT'D)	**Module 4** Prophetic Intercession in Worship Part 2	Prophetic Mantle The Power of Prophetic Worship in Prophetic Intercession Prophetic Sound as an Offensive Weapon Sharpening Your Spiritual Senses & Discernment	1-Page Report	Be able to identify 10 things that the power of prophetic worship and intercession is able to do.
	Module 5 Prophetic Intercession in Warfare Part 1	Spiritual Warfare Ministry of Deliverance Discerning & Dealing with Spiritual Atmospheres Understanding Your Level in Prophetic Intercession Understanding & Honoring Spiritual Tiers Understanding Your Spiritual Armor	1-Page Report Warfare Prayer	Define territorial spirits, identify them in their cities or churches, and create a warfare prayer.
	Module 6 Prophetic Intercession in Warfare Part 2	Identifying Territorial Spirits in Each State Warfare Strategies for Prophetic Intercessors	Warfare Prayer	Create another warfare prayer for another region or territory.

SPIRITUAL WARFARE STRATEGIES (CONT'D)	**Module 6** (cont'd)	Manifestations of Being Wounded in Battle		
SPHERES OF PROPHETIC INTERCESSION	**Module 7** Prophetic Intercession in the Marketplace Part 1	Applying Prophetic Intercession Principles to Create Solutions for the Marketplace	Project	Create a prophetic prayer for one (1) global challenge and one (1) current event in the marketplace.
	Module 8 Prophetic Intercession in the Marketplace Part 2	Presenting Projects & Receiving Feedback Principles of Creating Prophetic Prayers as Marketplace Solutions	None	None
	Module 9 Covering Apostolic & Prophetic Leaders via Prophetic Intercession Part 1	Apostolic Strength & Intercession Prophetic Decree Spirit of Momentum Power of Breakthrough, Decreeing, Utterance, & Clearing the Way	None	None
	Module 10 Covering Apostolic & Prophetic Leaders via Prophetic Intercession Part 2	Position of Authority Purity of Heart Prayer is Love Prayer Points to Cover Apostolic & Prophetic Leaders	Prophetic Declarations & Decrees	Create fifteen (15) prophetic declarations and decrees for their leaders.

PROPHETIC INTERCESSION ASSIGNMENT	**Module 11** Kingdom Results of Prophetic Intercession Part 1	Additional Prophetic Intercession Tips Test Preparation Prophetic Resources	None	None
	Module 12 Kingdom Results of Prophetic Intercession Part 2	Model of Live GICMP's Prophetic Prayer Line Training Calls	Prophetic Intercession Quiz	Take the prophetic intercession quiz.

LEADING IN:
FOCUS ON THE FACILITATOR

Rationale for a Facilitator-Focused Curriculum

*The appearance of the wheels and their craftsmanship
was like the gleam of beryl, and all four had the same form.
Their appearance and craftsmanship [were] like a wheel within a wheel.
Wherever the Spirit wanted to go, the creatures went in the direction
the Spirit was moving. The wheels rose alongside them,
for the spirit of the living creatures was in the wheels.
Ezek.1:16,20 (HCSB)*

Facilitators learn with their participants. They lead with a servant's heart and model the same expectation that they desire to see: a teachable spirit. Leaders and their ministries are a fitly joined unit where each person walks in agreement and uses his or her gifts to accomplish the vision (Eph. 4:16).

The facilitator-focused curriculum emphasizes leading by example through reflection and placing the Holy Spirit at the center of everything you do.

Before you begin this training, you need to *lead in*:

- ASSESS where you are.
- CREATE your vision.
- DEVISE a plan for facilitation.
- DEVELOP prayer points.
- REFLECT on where you are and where you want to be.

After the training ends, you need to *lead out*:

- EVALUATE your facilitation.
- ASSESS if you met your vision and prayer points.
- REFLECT on your steps in moving forward.

Curriculum Matrix for the Facilitator

	THE PROCESS	
LEADING IN: **FOCUS ON THE FACILITATOR** First Reflection Course Vision Course Planning Guide Prayer Points	Preparing the Facilitator to Lead: Focus on the Course 12 Module Overviews • Objectives • Key Terms • Key Concepts • Key Scriptures • Lesson Structure & Discussion Questions • Module Assignment & Rubric • Facilitation Strategies • Supplemental Exercises ⟵ CONTINUOUS REFLECTION AND PRAYER ⟶	**LEADING OUT:** **FOCUS ON THE FACILITATOR** Facilitator's Evaluation Final Reflection

First Reflection

Write your responses to the following reflective questions in your journal.

1. **Your Intimacy with God**
    a. Take a few moments to find a quiet place where you can hear God's voice. Write what you hear and see.

2. **Your Facilitation Skills**
    a. Ask the Holy Spirit how He wants you to facilitate. Pray for Him to reveal the needs of your church, city, or region.
    b. What are your thoughts about facilitating the training?
    c. What are you most excited about when you think about the upcoming training?
    d. What do you think will be the most challenging aspect of the upcoming training?
    e. What is your facilitation style?
    f. What are your strengths as a facilitator?
    g. Which areas of growth do you want to improve?
    h. Reflect on Gen.1:11 & 1Cor.3:6. What seeds of instruction can you plant through your facilitation? How do you perceive your role as a facilitator: to plant or to water? How will you self-assess your effectiveness?

3. **Your Foundation in Prophetic Intercession**
    a. How do you define prophetic intercession?
    b. What does that definition look like in action?
    c. How were you trained in prophetic intercession?
    d. What experiences from your journey can you share during this training?

4. **Your Lifestyle as a Prophetic Intercessor**
    a. What challenges are you facing?
    b. In which areas do you need to grow?
    c. In what areas do you need to increase in strength and stamina?
    d. What do you hope to gain from this course?

5. **Your Experiences in Prophetic Intercession**
    a. Reflect on Psalm 144:1-2a &14b. Think about the battles you have spiritually fought in your life. How did the Lord show Himself to be "a man of war" or Jehovah Gibbor during those times of spiritual warfare?
    b. What strategies, insights, experiences, and testimonies can you share with your participants?

    c. How does prophetic intercession cause major shifts in spiritual and earth realms? What experiences about shifts or transitions can you share?
    d. How can you connect your experiences to the principles of prophetic intercession taught in this course?

6. Your Ministry or Church
    a. What do you want your ministry or church to gain from this course?
    b. How do you envision this course as a tool to become a stronger and more effective ministry or church?
    c. What areas do you foresee needing further development?

7. Your Region
    a. What are the areas of need for your city, state, or region?
    b. How can this course help you meet those needs?

Course Vision

*If people can't see what God is doing, they stumble all over themselves.
But when they attend to what he reveals, they are most blessed.
Proverbs 29:18 (MSG)*

Reflect on the following prompts and respond to them in your journal.

1. Prepare to write your vision for this training by answering these questions:

    a. What is the Holy Spirit revealing to you?
    b. After taking this course, what changes or growth do you expect to see in your ministry or church?
    c. How do you envision this course helping you and your ministry or church to develop your effectiveness, strength, and stamina?
    d. What do you want prophetic intercession to look like in your ministry or church after completing this course?

2. Now write your vision statement.

3. List three (3) goals you want to accomplish by the end of this course.

4. What are the core values that define your ministry or church?

5. How do your vision statement, goals, and core values align with each other and this course?

Course Planning Guide

Reflect on the following information and write your course plan in your journal.

1st –Decide on Your Mode of Facilitation

- *Suggested Facilitation Mode:*

    Show the video and engage in discussion after viewing it.

- *Suggested Time Frame for Each Module:*

    The course is designed for you to cover the modules on a weekly or monthly basis.

- *Things to Consider during the Planning Phase:*

    This training manual provides you with module overviews. Each module overview has a lesson structure that outlines the order of activities in the video and includes additional discussion questions.

    Each module also has an assignment to complete (except for Modules 8, 9, and 11). There is a one-page assignment sheet that provides instructions and a rubric for grading. You have the option of printing the assignment sheet and distributing it to your participants.

    Ask yourself:

    a. Where am I going to conduct the training: face-to-face, Zoom, Google Meet, Microsoft Teams, Adobe Connect, etc.?
    b. What facilitation mode will work best for my ministry or church?
    c. What equipment and other materials do I need to run the training?
    d. Do I want to cover each module weekly, bi-weekly, or monthly?
    e. How much time do I want to schedule for each session?
    f. How often do I want to meet?
    g. How will my participants submit assignments to me?
    h. Do I want to give the key scriptures as a homework assignment before we begin each module?
    i. How will I assess mastery of each module?
    j. How do I want to handle our Q &A sessions and homework reviews? Do I want to discuss them before the video, after they take place in the video, or after the video has ended?

k. Do I want to find a platform that offers online discussions and have them engage in discussions virtually?
l. What type of prophetic intercession internship or post training opportunity will I implement for my ministry or church?

2nd –Decide on Materials for Your Ministry or Church

- *Things to Consider:*
    a. Journals
    b. Access to a computer, laptop, or mobile device
    c. Ask yourself:
        1. What else will my participants need to be successful in this training?
        2. What other systems do I need in place to facilitate effectively?

Prayer Points

It is important to pray targeted, effective prayers before, during, and after your training. Think of five (5) prayer points that you want to focus on while you facilitate. Write your prayer points, prayers, declarations, and decrees in your journal.

1st Prayer Point:_____

2nd Prayer Point:_____

3rd Prayer Point:_____

4th Prayer Point:_____

5th Prayer Point:_____

PREPARING THE FACILITATOR TO LEAD:
FOCUS ON THE COURSE

Module 1 Overview

Prophetic Intercession 101

Objectives

In this module, participants will

1. Understand these terms: *prophet*, *prophetic*, *prophetic intercession*, *regular intercession*, and *throne room*.

2. Identify the challenges of prophetic intercession.

3. Learn about the model of prophetic intercession and listen to an example.

4. Discuss how to rate their progression and growth in intercession.

5. Differentiate between regular intercession and prophetic intercession by researching examples in the scriptures.

Key Terms

Prophet
Prophetic
Prophetic Intercession

Additional Terms

Breach
Humbleness
Prayer Points
Regular Intercession
Synergy
Throne Room
Transition

Key Concepts

W. I. P. Model (**W**orship ~ **I**ntercession ~ **P**rophecy)

Avoiding Breaches in Prayer

Key Scriptures

Luke 2:36-37
1 Chr. 23:30
1 Chr. 25:1-3,5,7
Matt.5:9-13
Luke 11:2-4
Eph.2:1-7
Rev.4:10

Module 1 Lesson Structure

1. Begin with the following discussion questions:

    - What does prophetic intercession mean to you?
    - What do you expect its basic components to be?

    *Based on their responses, assess where they are and what you need to emphasize during the lesson.

2. Start Module 1 video.

3. Begin with prayer, introductions, and overview of the course.

4. Define the key terms: *prophet*, *prophetic*, and *prophetic intercession*.

5. Introduce Paula Price's *The Prophet's Dictionary* as a resource.

6. List key scriptures.

7. Ask the following discussion questions:

    - How do these three terms work together in a ministry or marketplace setting?
    - What do you think "supernatural communications, acts, and influences from the spiritual world" mean? Can you give an example?

8. Read and discuss Luke 2:36-37 and Luke 11:2-4.

9. Describe the three (3) challenges of prophetic intercession and give a solution to those challenges.

10. Present the W.I.P. Model and explain the connections to Luke 11:2-4.

11. Listen to a live recording of a W.I.P. Model demonstration.

12. Debrief the recording through summary and discussion.

13. Explain the homework assignment.

14. Provide time for Q&A.

- 1st Participant's Question in the Video: What exactly is hearing from the throne room?
- 2nd Participant's Question in the Video: How do you rate your progression and growth in intercession?

15. Ask this discussion question:
    - How can we use the W.I.P model in our ministry setting?

16. End in prayer.

17. Debrief the video.

Module 1 Assignment

Write a detailed, one-page report explaining the differences between regular intercession and prophetic intercession. Use several scriptural examples in your discussion.

Rubric		
Criteria	Met the Criteria (Y)	Did Not Meet the Criteria (N)
• Demonstrates understanding of regular intercession.		
• Demonstrates understanding of prophetic intercession.		
• Explains the difference between regular intercession and prophetic intercession.		
• Includes biblical references of regular intercession and prophetic intercession.		
• Meets the 1-page requirement.		

Facilitation Strategies

*Then opened he their understanding,
that they might understand the scriptures.
Luke 24:45*

1. Provide another W.I.P. Model demonstration with two of your seasoned prophetic intercessors. Use a prayer point that relates specifically to your ministry or church. Debrief and discuss with your participants.

2. If you are conducting the session on Zoom, you can also use breakout rooms. Divide your participants into groups and assign a current prayer point relevant to your ministry. Have each group practice prophetically praying over that prayer point. When everyone returns to the main room, ask each group to give feedback on the activity.

3. Discuss your current protocols for prophetic intercession and assess how they align with the W.I.P. model.

Supplemental Exercises

Finding the W.I.P. Model in Scripture

Take one of their prophetic intercession examples from their reports and identify the W.I.P. Model components. Instruct them to explain how it illustrates the definition of prophetic intercession.

Identifying Prayer Breaches

Have your participants research the word *breach* in the scriptures, identify breaches in the Bible, and explain how God used prophetic intercessors to repair them. Consider using Nehemiah as an example. Discuss how Jesus is the repairer of the breach in the relationship between God and man.

Module 2 Overview

The Lifestyle of a Prophetic Intercessor

Objectives

In this module, participants will

1. Understand what the term *lifestyle of a prophetic intercessor* means and the principles that describe it.

2. Know the importance of consecration, submission or yielding, worship, and faith in the prophetic intercessor's life.

3. Analyze the lifestyle of a prophetic intercessor in the Bible.

4. Reflect on how they are building their lifestyles as prophetic intercessors daily or weekly.

5. Identify challenges and areas of spiritual development in their lifestyles.

Key Terms

What a Prophetic Intercessor Needs
Clarity
Discernment
Faith
Insight
Power
Revelation
Wisdom

What a Prophetic Intercessor Maintains
Consecration
Holiness
Purity of Heart
Spiritual Sensitivity
Submission

Key Concepts

Intimacy with God

Lifestyle of Consecration and Holiness

Yield to the Holy Spirit

Key Scriptures

1 Pet.1:16
Heb.12:14
Rom.12:1
2 Tim. 2:21
Rev. 19:20
Judg.7:9-15
Gen. 22:1-18
Rom.10:17
James 4:2-14
Jer. 33:3
John 16:13
1 Cor.2:14

Module 2 Lesson Structure

1. Begin with the following discussion questions:

    - How would you define the lifestyle of a prophetic intercessor?
    - What does it look like?

    *Based on their responses, assess where they are and what you need to emphasize during the lesson.

2. Start Module 2 video.

3. Begin with prayer.

4. Review Module 1 homework. Decide whether you will review their homework before or after listening to the participants in the video.

5. Discuss the importance of having a strong relationship with God, hearing His voice clearly, and maintaining intimacy with Him.

6. Read 1 Pet.1:16 and Heb.12:14 and expand on the principles of the prophetic intercessor's lifestyle found in these verses.

7. Teach what it means to be consecrated, a living sacrifice, and a vessel of honor unto the Lord.

8. Read Rom.12:1 and 2 Tim. 2:21.

9. Ask the following discussion questions:

    - How does the traditional way that churches have viewed holiness differ from the way it is being defined in this module?
    - What can hinder you from hearing God's voice clearly?
    - What can cause your heart to become impure?

10. Introduce worship as a part of the prophetic intercessor's lifestyle.

11. Read Rev.19:20 and Judg.7:9-15.

12. List examples of what worship releases to the prophetic intercessor.

13. Describe the seven (7) qualities that must flow through the lifestyle of a prophetic intercessor.

14. Emphasize the importance of faith in the prophetic intercessor's lifestyle.

15. Read Rom.10:17.

16. Ask the following discussion questions:

    - If faith is like a muscle, how do you exercise or strengthen it daily?
    - What can weaken your faith?

17. Provide time for Q&A.

18. Explain the homework assignment.

19. End in prayer.

20. Debrief the video.

Module 2 Assignment

The written assignment for this module has three main components:

1. *Reflective Self-Assessment*
   Examine and share how you are building your lifestyle as a prophetic intercessor daily or weekly.

2. *Action Plan*
   Identify three (3) challenges you face as a prophetic intercessor and three (3) things you will do now to increase your strength as an intercessor.

3. *Application*
   Find a prophetic intercessor in the Bible and describe what makes him or her a solid prophetic intercessor.

Rubric		
Criteria	Met the Criteria (Y)	Did Not Meet the Criteria (N)
• Gives specific examples of how they are building their prophetic intercessory lifestyles.		
• Identifies three (3) challenges that they face as intercessors.		
• States three (3) things to increase their strength as intercessors.		
• Identifies a prophetic intercessor in the Bible and explains how he or she is strong intercessor using the principles from this module.		

Facilitation Strategies

*Then opened he their understanding,
that they might understand the scriptures.
Luke 24:45*

1. Have your participants reflect on the current state of their lifestyles as prophetic intercessors. What spiritual practices are they implementing into their devotional lives? How are they building their intercessory lifestyles, and what are they using to build them? What is the current state of their hearts? Have them think about how often they practice building their intercessory lifestyles: daily, weekly, or intermittently. Ask them to share their responses at the beginning of the next session.

2. Assess the state of your intercessory prayer team or ministry. Have you been on target and effective in your assignments?

3. Set aside time for recalibration and realignment as a team. Seek the Lord for strategies and insight. Ask the Holy Spirit if you need to fast corporately. You may even think about organizing a type of prayer retreat that involves sitting in silence in the presence of the Lord and listening for His direction.

Supplemental Exercise

Addressing the Spirit of Faint

Have participants look up scriptures on the word *faint* and explain the promises and strategies God gives to deal with this affliction. Ask them to find an example of a prophetic intercessor or prophet who battles with the spirit of faint or weariness and explain how the Lord refreshes and strengthens him or her. Have them reflect and write about how the spirit of faint or weariness can affect their lifestyles as prophetic intercessors. Instruct them to ask the Lord to give them strength and stamina, reveal and repair any damage to their spiritual armor, and loose the spirit of endurance.

Module 3 Overview

Prophetic Intercession in Worship Part 1

Objectives

In this module, participants will

1. Understand these terms: *prophetic declaration*, *decree*, and *prophetic worship*.

2. Identify key principles of prophetic worship.

3. Explain the relationship between prophetic worship and prophetic intercession.

Key Terms

Prophetic Declaration & Decree
Prophetic Worship

Additional Terms

Shifting
Song of the Lord
Spiritual Communion
Spiritual Intelligence
Zeal (Passion for God)

Key Concepts

The Power of Prophetic Worship
in Prophetic Intercession

Prophetic Worship as a Bridge

Prophetic Worship as a Weapon

Key Scripture

2 Chr.20:1-30

Module 3 Lesson Structure

1. Begin with the following discussion questions:

    - How would you describe prophetic worship?
    - Do you think there is a connection between prophetic worship and prophetic intercession? Why or why not?

    *Based on their responses, assess where they are and what you need to emphasize during the lesson.

2. Start Module 3 video.

3. Address general housekeeping activities related to the course (i.e. roll call)

4. Begin with prayer.

5. Review Module 2 homework. Decide whether you will review their homework before or after listening to the participants in the video.

6. Define the key terms: *prophetic declaration*, *decree*, and *prophetic worship*.

7. Read and discuss 2 Chr.20:1-24.

8. Explain the power of fasting and share principles of prophetic worship and its connection to prophetic intercession shown in the scriptures.

9. Pause for questions and/or comments.

10. Ask the following discussion questions:

    - Discuss your takeaways from the module so far.
    - How do you engage in worship?
    - Prophet Renee discusses a personal experience in which she had to shift in the spirit realm and prophetically intercede for her child. Has there ever been a time when you had to prophetically war in the spirit for a loved one? Share your experience.

    *This would be a great opportunity for you to share one of your experiences as a teaching moment.

11. Read and discuss 2 Chr. 20:25-30.

12. Present additional principles of prophetic worship and its connection to prophetic intercession.

13. Provide time for Q&A.

14. Explain the homework assignment.

15. Ask the following discussion questions:

    a. What is the difference between regular worship and prophetic worship? Is there a difference between them?
    b. Think about a problem or situation that you have had. How did you maintain standing still?

16. End in prayer.

17. Debrief the video.

Module 3 Assignment

Get a topic or situation and pray it through in prophetic intercession. It can be a current event or a situation in your own life. Use the principles taught in this module. Share the insights and strategies God gives you. Be prepared to share scriptures to support what you prophetically prayed. Reflect on this assignment in your journal.

Rubric		
Criteria	Met the Criteria (Y)	Did Not Meet the Criteria (N)
• Identifies the topic or situation.		
• Engages in prophetic intercession and prophetic worship for the topic or situation.		
• Makes prophetic declarations and decrees regarding the topic or situation.		
• Includes scriptures to back up what they are prophetically praying.		
• Shares insights and strategies God gave them.		

Facilitation Strategies

*Then opened he their understanding,
that they might understand the scriptures.
Luke 24:45*

1. This lesson is full of prophetic insight and strategies about prophetic intercession in worship. You may want to consider extending the duration of time spent on this module. Emphasize the strong connection between prophetic worship and prophetic intercession.

2. Find an appropriate time during the lesson to stop the video and engage in prophetic worship and intercession together. You may even want to set up additional times to practice these principles.

3. Encourage your participants to be intentional in incorporating extra time for prophetic worship for the next two weeks. Ask them to reflect on the experiences in their journals and share any insights or changes they have noticed.

4. Discuss your current protocols for worship and assess how well you have been able to shift during worship and prophetic intercession.

5. You may want to ask them to write or record their prayers, declarations, and decrees. Decide how you are going to give them feedback on this assignment. You need to gauge where they are and how well they are applying the principles. As you move forward through the modules, the complexity of the assignments will increase. It is important to have clarity about this module's principles.

Supplemental Exercise

Finding Biblical Examples of Prophetic Worship

Find examples of prophetic worship in the Bible and discuss what happens during and after prophetic worship. Have them look for patterns and principles of prophetic worship and prophetic intercession in their examples.

Module 4 Overview

Prophetic Intercession in Worship Part 2

Objectives

In this module, participants will

1. Review what prophetic worship releases.

2. Learn additional principles about the power of prophetic worship in prophetic intercession.

3. Realize the power of sound and its ability to synchronize and release in the spirit.

4. List ten (10) examples of what the power of prophetic worship and intercession is able to do.

Key Terms

Prophetic Mantle
Prophetic Sound
Prophetic Worship

Key Concepts

The Power of Prophetic Worship
in Prophetic Intercession

Prophetic Sound as an Offensive Weapon

Sharpening Your Spiritual Senses & Discernment

Key Scriptures

1 Sam.10:5-11
1 Cor. 2:9-10
2 Chr. 7:1
Dan. 9:21-23
Luke 1:10-11
Luke 3:21-23
Acts 4:31
Psa.149:6-9

Additional Scriptures

2 Cor. 3:18
2 Pet. 1:4
Dan. 10
Rev. 19:10

Module 4 Lesson Structure

1. Begin with the following discussion questions:

   - We have heard prophetic worship being described as a bridge and a weapon. How would you describe the relationship between prophetic worship and prophetic intercession?
   - For example, prophetic intercession is like the bow that prophetic intercessors hold in their hands. Prophetic worship is like the arrows they have in the bag to draw, aim, and shoot.
   - Another example is prophetic worship is like the rocks David had in his bag. The right prophetic sound hit the target and dismantled Goliath's stronghold of fear and intimidation against Israel.
   - You could also do an object lesson as a review by having different objects laid out on a table and asking them to pick two items. One item will represent prophetic worship. The other item will represent prophetic intercession. Each person will give a demonstration of the relationship between prophetic worship and prophetic intercession using the objects.

2. Start Module 4 video.

3. Begin with prayer.

4. Review Module 3 homework. Decide whether you will review their homework before or after listening to the participants in the video.

5. List key scriptures for this module.

6. Explain thirteen (13) principles of prophetic worship in prophetic intercession using different key scriptures from the above list.

7. Share a specific example of how prophetic worship in intercession revealed a level of understanding, insight, and strategy in a personal situation.

8. Provide time for Q &A.

9. Ask the following discussion questions:

    - How is prophetic sound a weapon in prophetic intercession?
    - How is stirring up your spirit connected to sharpening your spiritual senses and discernment?
    - Describe a time where you have experienced angelic assistance.

10. Connect Q &A discussion to the principles and scriptures discussed in the module. Mention Rev.19:10 as a scriptural foundation to the principles being taught in this lesson.

11. Review Luke1:10-11 and discuss additional principles of prophetic intercession in worship.

12. Stress the most important principle to remember: The greatest worship offered to the Lord involves just yielding to His voice.

13. Ask the following discussion question:

    - What are your major takeaways from the Q &A session?

14. Explain the homework assignment.

15. End in prayer.

16. Debrief the video.

Module 4 Assignment

Write a detailed, one-page report sharing ten (10) things that the **power of prophetic intercession and worship** is able to do. Use several scriptural examples in your discussion.

Rubric		
Criteria	Met the Criteria (Y)	Did Not Meet the Criteria (N)
• Discusses ten (10) things that the power of prophetic intercession and worship is able to do.		
• Includes at least one (1) scripture for each of the ten (10) things listed.		
• Demonstrates a clear understanding of the concept.		
• Meets the 1-page requirement.		

Facilitation Strategies

*Then opened he their understanding,
that they might understand the scriptures.
Luke 24:45*

1. Have them practice the power of prophetic sound as an offensive weapon. Provide additional opportunities to engage in prophetic worship and intercession during this video.

2. Discuss the power and importance of accessing the glory realm in prophetic intercession.

3. Read 1 Sam.19:19-24 and discuss the verses using the principles of this module.

Supplemental Exercise

Principles and Protocols of Angelic Assistance

Find examples in the Bible where people had encounters with angels. Discuss five (5) principles and protocols these biblical examples teach about the right way to handle angelic assistance.

Module 5 Overview

Prophetic Intercession in Warfare Part 1

Objectives

In this module, participants will

1. Discover a new strategy in making declarations.

2. Understand several key terms related to spiritual warfare.

3. Gain new insight on spiritual armor and its role in prophetic intercession and spiritual warfare.

4. Be able to discern and deal with spiritual atmospheres during prophetic intercession.

5. Learn about spiritual tiers and other basic principles of prophetic intercession in warfare.

6. Create a warfare prayer for their cities or churches.

Key Terms

What Prophetic Intercessors Engage
Ministry of Deliverance
Spiritual Warfare

What Prophetic Intercessors Must Understand
Spirit of Truth
Discerning of Spirits
Spiritual Armor & Spiritual Atmosphere

How the Enemy Camp is Organized
Spiritual Tiers
Powers, Principalities, & Territorial Spirits
Rulers of Darkness of This World
Spiritual Wickedness in High Places

Exposing the Enemy's Devices (2 Cor.2:11)
Witchcraft
Occult Activity
New Age Movement
Apostolic & Prophetic Witchcraft

Key Concepts

Discerning and Dealing with Spiritual Atmospheres

Understanding Your Level in Prophetic Intercession

Understanding and Honoring Spiritual Tiers

Understanding Your Spiritual Armor

Key Scriptures

Dan.10:12-21
Psa.37:1-8
Dan. 9-11
Eph.6:12-20
Psa. 91
Rev.12:11

Module 5 Lesson Structure

1. Begin with the following discussion questions:

    - What is the ministry of deliverance?
    - How do you define spiritual warfare?
    - What kinds of spiritual warfare have you been noticing in our church, city, in the news, and/or globally?

    *Based on their responses, assess where they are and what you need to emphasize during the lesson.

2. Start Module 5 video.

3. Begin with prayer.

4. Review Module 4 Homework. Decide whether you will review their homework before or after listening to the participants in the video.

5. Use one of the scriptures from the Power of Prophetic Intercession and Worship homework assignment and make a declaration.

6. Discuss the strategy of taking scriptures and making declarations from them. Show how this strategy can shift atmospheres, especially in situations where tongues are not received. Give the example of declaring Psalm 91. Stress the importance of declaring with a level of authority and power.

7. Listen to a demonstration of the strategy using Psa. 37:8 and discuss the principles that they can apply from this demonstration.

8. Read Dan.10:12-21 (MSG) and Eph.6:12-20 (KJV).

9. Introduce key terms: *ministry of deliverance* and *spiritual warfare*.

10. Share basic principles of prophetic intercession in warfare.

11. Introduce the term *spiritual tiers* through Eph.6:12 & Eph.4:11.

12. Present the principles of prophetic intercession in warfare in Eph.6:12-20.

13. Ask the following discussion questions:

    - What new insights do you have about your spiritual armor?
    - How does cleaning the spiritual armor relate to the spirit of faint and weariness?
    - Are there any other questions or comments?

14. Discuss the principles of prophetic intercession in warfare in Dan.10:12-21.

15. List additional key terms for research.

16. Explain the homework assignment.

17. Provide time for Q & A.

18. List three (3) principles about the importance of fruit in prophetic intercession.

19. End in prayer.

20. Ask the following discussion question:

    - How can these principles of prophetic intercession in warfare help us to become a more effective ministry or church?

21. Debrief the video.

Module 5 Assignment

The written assignment for this module has three main components:

1. *Defining the Concept*
   Define territorial spirits.

2. *Identifying the Concept*
   Identify the territorial spirits that are plaguing your city, hometown, church, etc.

3. *Applying the Concept*
   Create a warfare prayer for your city or church.

Rubric		
Criteria	Met the Criteria (Y)	Did Not Meet the Criteria (N)
• Defines the term territorial spirits.		
• Identifies the territorial spirits plaguing their cities, hometowns, etc.		
• Creates a warfare prayer (including scripture-based declarations and decrees) for their cities or churches.		
• Incorporates principles of prophetic intercession in warfare taught in this module.		
• Meets the 1-page requirement.		

Facilitation Strategies

*Then opened he their understanding,
that they might understand the scriptures.
Luke 24:45*

1. This module includes in-depth discussion of warfare strategies. You may want to schedule more than one session to cover this module. The terminology is complex, but it is knowledge in which prophetic intercessors should demonstrate understanding as they proceed to the next module.

2. Have your participants find scriptural examples of people in the Bible engaging in the principles of prophetic intercession in warfare.

3. Encourage them to reflect on the current state of their spiritual armor and their levels and spiritual tiers in prophetic intercession. They should write their responses in their journals.

Supplemental Exercise

Defining Additional Key Terms

This module only defined ministry of deliverance and spiritual warfare. Have them research the remaining key terms listed in this overview and find scriptural references for the terms. They will define the key terms, discuss scriptures that support each term, and write a reflection on what they have found. It is highly suggested that you assign this exercise.

Module 6 Overview

Prophetic Intercession in Warfare Part 2

Objectives

In this module, participants will

1. Review *ministry of deliverance*, *spiritual warfare*, and *territorial spirits*.

2. Learn warfare strategies in prophetic intercession.

3. Identify manifestations of being wounded in battle.

4. Practice creating additional warfare prayers.

Key Terms

Ministry of Deliverance
Spiritual Warfare

Additional Terms

Battle Wounds (Isa.1:5-6)
Cycles

Key Concepts

What Prophetic Intercessors Need
During Spiritual Warfare

Manifestations of Being Wounded in Battle

Identifying Territorial Spirits in Each State

Key Scriptures

John 12:31
Eph.6:12-20
Psa.91:1-4

Module 6 Lesson Structure

1. Begin with the following discussion question:
   - What promises of God do you stand on during spiritual warfare?

2. Start Module 6 video.

3. Begin with roll call and prayer.

4. Review Module 5 Homework. Decide whether you will review their homework before or after listening to the participants in the video.

5. Discuss territorial spirits in Florida, Maryland, and Georgia.

6. Introduce *Releasing the Prophetic Destiny of a Nation* by Dutch Sheets and Chuck D. Pierce as a resource.

7. Review the terms *ministry of deliverance* and *spiritual warfare*.

8. Read John12:31-33 (KJV & MSG) & Eph.6:12-20 (KJV).

9. Present principles of prophetic intercession in spiritual warfare.

10. List three (3) things prophetic intercessors need in spiritual warfare.

11. Ask the following discussion questions:
    - What strategic game plan or course(s) of action should we take to intercede effectively for our church or region?
    - How can we more effectively set the atmosphere in our church before our spiritual leader brings the message?

12. Read and discuss Psalm 91:1-4.

13. Give five (5) manifestations of being wounded in battle.

14. Provide time for Q&A.

15. Impart more warfare strategies in prophetic intercession.

16. End in prayer.

17. Explain homework assignment.

18. Debrief the video.

Module 6 Assignment

This written assignment gives you more practice with engaging in strategic prophetic intercession in spiritual warfare. Create another warfare prayer for your ministry, church, or another region.

Rubric		
Criteria	Met the Criteria (Y)	Did Not Meet the Criteria (N)
• Creates a warfare prayer for their cities, ministries, churches or another region.		
• Makes scripture-based declarations and decrees.		
• Incorporates principles of prophetic intercession in warfare taught in this module.		
• Meets the 1-page requirement.		

Facilitation Strategies

*Then opened he their understanding,
that they might understand the scriptures.
Luke 24:45*

1. While you are reviewing Module 5 homework, you may want to give a scriptural example of a territorial spirit (Acts 16:16-19). During the homework review in the video, Prophet Renee discusses territorial spirits in Florida, Maryland, and Georgia. Discuss other examples of territorial spirits in different regions.

2. Choose a territorial spirit that you discern is coming against your church, ministry, or region. Create a list of 3-5 points of attack and assign one to different intercessors. Engage in warfare prayer together. This activity can be done during or after the video.

3. Keep track of the territorial spirits that are mentioned during your discussion. Seek the Lord for warfare strategies and collaborate with your participants to create strategic battle plans and courses of action.

Supplemental Exercises

Exploring the Manifestations of Being Wounded in Battle

Have participants research the following manifestations mentioned in the module: lack, oppression, depression, infirmity, and no fruit. Find biblical references and explain the insights and strategies God reveals. Reflect on any personal experiences with these cycles.

Fighting for Your Families

Reflect on generational, familiar, or territorial spirits that are plaguing your families. Seek the Lord for insight and strategies and create a warfare prayer.

Module 7 Overview

Prophetic Intercession in the Marketplace Part 1

Objectives

In this module, participants will

1. Discuss opportunities for internships or prophetic intercession practice specifically for your ministry or church.

2. Learn about their projects.

3. Share testimonies and give general feedback on progress in the course.

Key Concept

Applying Prophetic Intercession Principles
to Create Solutions for the Marketplace

Module 7 Lesson Structure

1. Start Module 7 video. ***Note:** You will experience a few moments of silence in the beginning of the video. The video will continue shortly.

2. Discuss availability to meet about their interest in internships. ***Note:** This is a great time to discuss internships or other opportunities your church will provide for participants to put the prophetic intercession principles into practice.

3. Share testimonies.

4. Discuss project.

5. End in prayer.

6. Debrief the video.

Module 7 Assignment

Prophetic Intercession in the Marketplace Project

- Choose one (1) Global Challenge in the Marketplace.
- Choose one (1) Current Event in the Marketplace.
- Create a Prophetic Prayer that Declares a Solution.
- Submit the Prophetic Prayer as a 1-Page Document.
- Be prepared to pray this prayer at the next training session.

Rubric		
Criteria	Met the Criteria (Y)	Did Not Meet the Criteria (N)
• Identifies one (1) global challenge in the marketplace.		
• Identifies one (1) current event in the marketplace.		
• Creates a prophetic prayer that declares a solution for the selected global challenge and current event in the marketplace.		
• Includes scripture-based declarations and decrees.		
• Incorporates the principles taught in Modules 1-6.		
• Meets the 1-page requirement.		

Facilitation Strategies

*Then opened he their understanding,
that they might understand the scriptures.
Luke 24:45*

1. Decide whether you want your participants to work independently on their projects or get feedback from each other. Give time for them to discuss their projects with you.

2. You may want to model an example of what you expect to see. One suggestion is to choose one (1) global challenge and one (1) current event from your marketplace industry or one related to your city. As a team, you and your participants create and pray the prophetic prayer for those prayer points.

3. Since the primary focus is on the project, it is suggested that no supplemental exercises are assigned.

Module 8 Overview

Prophetic Intercession in the Marketplace Part 2

Objectives

In this module, participants will

1. Present their prophetic intercession in the marketplace projects.

2. Receive feedback on their projects.

3. Learn effective strategies for praying prophetically in the marketplace.

Key Concept

Principles on Creating Prophetic Prayers
as Marketplace Solutions

Module 8 Lesson Structure

1. Start Module 8 video.

2. Listen to participants present projects.

3. Give feedback on what they did.

4. Introduce principles on creating prophetic prayers as marketplace solutions.

5. Provide time for Q &A and testimonies.

6. End with prayer.

7. Debrief the video.

No Module 8 Assignment

Facilitation Strategies

*Then opened he their understanding,
that they might understand the scriptures.
Luke 24:45*

1. Have participants pray their prayers before watching the video and give them feedback. Then watch the video and discuss it.

2. Provide another opportunity to practice praying prophetically for marketplace solutions as a group.

3. After this session, assess where your participants are. Determine if you need to assign additional practice with creating prophetic prayers as marketplace solutions or creating warfare prayers.

Module 9 Overview

Covering Apostolic & Prophetic Leaders via Prophetic Intercession Part 1

Objectives

In this module, participants will

1. Understand these terms: momentum, decree, discernment, breakthrough, apostolic strength and intercession, and authority.

2. Learn the principles of covering apostolic and prophetic leaders in prophetic intercession.

3. Discuss the spirit of momentum, the power of breakthrough, the power of decreeing and utterance, and the power of clearing the way.

Key Terms

Momentum
Decree
Discernment
Breakthrough
Authority
Apostolic Strength
Apostolic Intercession

Key Concepts

Spirit of Momentum
Power of Breakthrough
Power of Decreeing & Utterance
Power of Clearing the Way

Key Scriptures

Eph.3:14-21
Psa.51:10

Additional Scriptures

Acts 4:31
Job 22:23
Josh.6

Module 9 Lesson Structure

1. Begin with the following discussion question:

    - Name some effective ways that prophetic intercessors can cover their leaders in prayer.

    *Based on their responses, assess where they are and what you need to emphasize during the lesson.

2. Start Module 9 video.

3. Announce prophetic counseling phone line.

4. Read and discuss Eph.3:14-21 and Psa.51:10.

5. Introduce six (6) principles for covering apostolic and prophetic leaders.

6. Explain the key concepts.

7. Define the key terms.

8. Provide time for Q &A.

9. Ask this discussion question:
    - How do you sensitize yourself to be properly discerning without being suspicious?

10. End in prayer.

11. Debrief the video.

No Module 9 Assignment

Facilitation Strategies

*Then opened he their understanding,
that they might understand the scriptures.
Luke 24:45*

1. Provide an opportunity for them to cover your pastor, apostolic/prophetic leaders, or spiritual/ministry leaders in prophetic intercession.

2. No supplemental exercises are given for this module. You may ask them to write a reflection in their journals.

Module 10 Overview

Covering Apostolic & Prophetic Leaders via Prophetic Intercession Part 2

Objectives

In this module, participants will

1. Review and learn additional principles of covering their apostolic and prophetic leaders in prophetic intercession.

2. Create fifteen (15) prophetic declarations and decrees for their leaders.

Key Concepts

Position of Authority

Purity in Heart

Prayer is Love

Key Scriptures

Eph.5:15-17
Exo.17:8-15

Module 10 Lesson Structure

1. Start Module 10 video.

2. Review principles and concepts of covering apostolic and prophetic leaders in prophetic intercession.

3. Introduce specific prayer points for apostolic and prophetic leaders.

4. Ask the following discussion questions:

   - What are your thoughts on these prayer points?
   - Which ones have you specifically covered in prophetic intercession?

5. Share additional principles on covering apostolic and prophetic leaders in prophetic intercession.

6. Provide time for Q & A.

7. Explain the homework assignment.

8. End in prayer.

9. Debrief the video.

Module 10 Assignment

Write fifteen (15) scripture-based apostolic and prophetic decrees and declarations for your leaders.

Rubric		
Criteria	Met the Criteria (Y)	Did Not Meet the Criteria (N)
• Writes fifteen (15) apostolic and prophetic decrees and declarations for their leaders.		
• Bases prophetic declarations and decrees on scriptures.		
• Incorporates principles of prophetic intercession from the modules.		

Facilitation Strategies

*Then opened he their understanding,
that they might understand the scriptures.
Luke 24:45*

1. Provide time to practice praying prophetically over your leaders using any of the prayer points introduced in the module.

2. No other supplemental exercises are recommended. The primary focus should be on developing their prophetic declarations and decrees for their leaders.

Module 11 Overview

Kingdom Results of Prophetic Intercession Part 1

Objectives

In this module, participants will

1. Have an opportunity to catch up on missing homework assignments.
2. Receive test preparation.
3. Learn additional tips on prophetic intercession.

Key Resources

GICMP Prophetic Convocation

GICMP Prophetic Prayer Explosion

PAQ (Prophetic Assessment Questionnaire)

MAQ (Ministry Assessment Questionnaire)

Prophetic Bootcamp

GICMP Ordination Track

Module 11 Lesson Structure

1. Start Module 11 video.
2. Discuss importance of submitting any missing homework assignments.
3. Present information on test preparation.
4. Give additional tips on prophetic intercession.
5. Mention prophetic resources.
6. Debrief the video.

No Module 11 Assignment

<u>Facilitation Strategies</u>

1. Decide how you will handle test preparation and what additional information you want to address before the final module.

2. No supplemental exercises are suggested.

Module 12 Overview

Kingdom Results of Prophetic Intercession Part 2

Objectives

In this module, participants will

1. Listen to live training calls from GICMP's Prophetic Prayer Line.
2. Take the Prophetic Intercession Quiz.

Key Resource

GICMP's Prophetic Intercession Internship Program

(6-month minimum commitment)

Module 12 Lesson Structure

1. Begin with the following discussion questions:
    - What are your major takeaways from this course?
    - Would anyone like to share any testimonies?

2. Start Module 12 video.

3. Discuss protocol for handling GICMP's Prophetic Prayer line (prophetic intercession, prophetic prayer, and deliverance calls).

4. Listen to live training calls and debrief them.

5. Provide time for Q & A.

6. End In prayer.

7. Debrief the video.

Module 12 Assignment

Take the Prophetic Intercession Quiz.

Facilitation Strategies

*Then opened he their understanding,
that they might understand the scriptures.
Luke 24:45*

1. Discuss your plans for prophetic internships or additional opportunities for your ministry to engage in prophetic intercession assignments.

2. Think about how you can incorporate the prophetic training model into your own ministry or church protocols.

3. Take care of any other ministry-related initiatives.

4. Celebrate everyone's spiritual growth and completion of the course!

LEADING OUT:
FOCUS ON THE FACILITATOR

Facilitator's Evaluation

Write your responses to the following questions in your journal.

1. What are your major takeaways from the training?
2. What went well during your facilitation of the course?
3. What are some areas of improvement in terms of facilitation?
4. What do you wish you could have done differently?
5. What kind of feedback did you receive from your team?
6. What changes would you make to the mode of facilitation?
7. Did you try any of the facilitation strategies or supplemental exercises? How did they go? Which ones would you adapt?
8. How well did you maintain your focus on your vision during the training?
9. How well did you meet your goals and prayer targets?
10. How well did you align your training to your core values?

Final Reflection

Write your thoughts in your journal.

1. Find a quiet place so you can hear God's voice. Ask Him for direction on moving forward with your ministry team. Write what you see and hear.

2. Reread your first reflection that you completed before you began facilitating the course. What has changed since you have written it? How have you grown spiritually? Reflect on your facilitation journey and record your thoughts.